Also by E. Reid Gilbert

Whimsical Limericks from the age of Trump

100 Limericks for 100 Days of Trump

Stories Tell What Can't be Told: My Story

Shall We Gather at the River

What Matters

Valley Studio: More than a Place

The Twelve Houses of My Childhood

Trickster Jack

E. Reid Gilbert Ten Plays

100 Limericks
for the
Final 100 Days
of
Trump

As Observed by
E. Reid Gilbert

A3D Impressions
Tucson | Minneapolis

100 Limericks for the Final 100 Days of Trump

Copyright © 2021 E. Reid Gilbert. All rights reserved. No part of this book may be reproduced or retransmitted in any form or by any means without the written permission of the publisher.

Published by

A3D Impressions©
P.O. Box 57415, Tucson, AZ 85735
www.a3dimpressions.com
a3dimpressions@gmail.com

Publisher's Cataloging-in-Publication data

Names: Gilbert, E. Reid, author.
Title: 100 Limericks for the final 100 days of Trump / E. Reid Gilbert.
Description: Tucson, AZ; Minneapolis, MN: A3D Impressions.
Identifiers: LCCN: 2021936500 |
ISBN: 978-1-7344724-8-6 (paperback) | 978-1-7344724-9-3 (ebook)
Subjects: LCSH Limericks. | Trump, Donald, 1946---Humor. | Presidents--United States--Humor. | Liberalism--United States--Humor. | Conservatism--United States--Humor. | Democratic Party (U.S.)--Humor. | Republican Party (U.S. : 1854-)--Humor. | BISAC POETRY / Subjects & Themes / General | HUMOR / Topic / Politics
Classification: LCC PN6231.P6 G55 2021 | DDC 320.9730207--dc23

LCCN: 2021936500
ISBN: 978-1-7344724-8-6 (paperback)
ISBN: 978-1-7344724-9-3 (ebook)

Donn Poll, cover and book design

Dedicated to Barbara Banks who has encouraged and supported my efforts all the way from the writing to the final production of the book. It would not have been possible without her input Barbara, my thanks.

The Limericks

In descending order.

Day 104   10/8/2020

I'd like to acknowledge that this is day 104
Before Trump retires to his tower top floor;
   But maybe serving time
   For his pernicious crimes,
Locked up with no key for the jailhouse door.

Day 103   10/9/2020

In the countdown, today should be about 103
When we from Trump will finally be free,
   To enjoy a democracy
   Instead of an aristocracy
Of Trump and his narcissistic hypocrisy.

Day 102   10/10/2020

Trump is now in a state of utter desperation,
As exhibited in his recent statements to the nation.
　Not to serve,
　But to swerve
From what awaits him...his certain incarceration.

101 Days   10/11/2020

Trump's not God, even though he says he is.
He flunked big time the divinity quiz.
  With several interruptions
  Known as bankruptions
He's now not known as a business whiz.

100 Days   10/12/2020

Today is Trump's countdown to the end of the dance.
Knowing his crimes deserve more than a mere glance,
    He's in a mental haze
    Facing his last 100 days,
Though he's hoping for another divine chance.

99 Days   10/11/2020

99 limericks of Trump on the wall.
If one of those 99 limericks should fall...
    Trump would be bereft
    Of all those still left.
And the game would be over, after all.

Day 98   10/12/2020

Today was scheduled to be the presidential
    debate.
So, Biden took note of this potentially important
    date.
    Not dropping the ball,
    He scheduled a town hall,
So, his plans he could outline and would
    articulate.

Day 97   10/15/2020

Although Trump backed out of the second debate,
He set up his town hall on the same time and date.
　When asked then
　If he didn't win,
He filled this political opportunity with vitriolic hate.

Day 96   10/16/2020

Ninety-six days left in this presidential
    countdown
When we'll be finished with this bumbling clown.
    Truth was the tool
    Of King Lear's fool
Something unknown as Trump wants a crown.

Day 95   10/17/2020

Last night we saw a wonderful pictorial
    documentary
Of a presidential presence quite extraordinary.
    I speak of course
    Without remorse
Of Obama, a president who was an empathic
    visionary.

The nation finds it absolutely essential
To have a president who is presidential,
    But not unnerving
    Like Trump's self-serving.
Obama's presidency was quite providential.

Day 94   10/18/2020

Trump insists on continuing his political rallies
But he completely ignores the need to tally
　The local expenses
　Of his and Pence's.
He assuredly does not leave with "Peace in the Valley."

Day 93   10/19/2020

Of the pandemic, Dr. Fauci is speaking out.
White House control is what it's about
  Though mysterious
  It's quite serious,
So, he felt it important to give a shout out.

Day 92   10/20/2020

It's now only two weeks until the election
When we'll find out the nation's direction.
   Hoping Trump will go
   And so will his show
Of self-serving greed and presidential desecration.

Day 91   10/21/2020

After Trump attempted to abolish the U S Mail,
He set out again on the campaign trail.
His Amy Barrett nomination
Was with the expectation
That eventually she would avoid his going to jail.

Day 90   10/22/2020

Trump must answer for his presidential crimes.
He even wants to play president overtime.
   He will be held accountable
   For misdeeds insurmountable.
The truth will truly trump Trump's lies over time.

Day 89   10/21/2020

In the debate Trump said one thing that was true.
Saying, "I know much more about wind than you."
To our despair
All his hot air
Ironically chills to the bone through and through.

Day 88   10/22/2020

Trump sought political support from foreign domains.
Israel's Prime Minister thought he had made it quite plain,
As Trump asked Bibi to widen
His base and speak against Biden,
But Bibi refused to endorse Trump's presidential campaign.

Day 87   10/23/2020

Trump accuses "fake news" as spreading COVID 19 fear
Of all people to accuse others as political profiteers
　TRUMP is the most
　Likely to boast
That if you listen to him the pandemic will soon disappear.

Day 86   10/26/2020

Today Amy Barrett joins Trump's regal regime,
To add to the total regression of his political
  machine.
  As she's now on the Court,
  What more to report,
That we need for a memorable mean Halloween?

Day 85   10/27/2020

Trump said, "I'm not going to control the pandemic."
With his head in the sand, ignoring this epidemic.
It's then that Trump
Shows his big rump,
Though his presidential plans are thin and anemic.

Day 84   10/28/2020

Trump now brags he stopped covid-19
At his mask-less rallies he prances and preens.
    He continues his rants,
    As well as his chants,
Hoping we'll forget his assaults as a libertine.

Day 83   10/29/2020

If Biden becomes president to the nation,
Trump said there would be an assassination
　In the first three weeks,
　And so, he speaks,
Giving his followers a badly hidden murder invitation.

Day 82   10/30/2020

Vote for only one: Trump or democracy
Choosing Trump, you'll also get his hypocrisy.
  I'll stake my oath
  That you can't have both.
Trump has already attempted a self-serving
    autocracy.

Day 81   10/31/2020

The election approaches in this really ghostly time
Trump will call, "Fraud", without reason or rhyme.
   As today is Halloween,
   Goblins will be seen.
One ghoul may be unable to escape his own slime.

Day 80   11/1/2020

In two more days, our nation will have decided,
Who will lead us from the morass that has
    divided
  Us into separate camps,
  Without lighted lamps,
But enough light to realize we have been
    blind-sided.

Day 79   11/2/2020

Tomorrow, American voting rights will be
　　applied,
When the nation tells Trump where to reside.
　　If not the White House,
　　He will certainly grouse,
But it's a matter in which he has nothing to
　　decide.

There are other places where he may be sent;
Not usual places for an ex-president
　　He won't be seen
　　In his usual limousine,
But attention in a spectacular media event.

Day 78   11/3/2020

Today is a crucial day for the future of our
    nation.
So, we cast our vote with hope and great
    expectation.
   Joyfully or with sorrow
   We'll only know tomorrow.
The ability to vote at all is a cause for celebration.

Day 77   11/4/2020

It's already tomorrow, and we still don't know.
This limerick project has lost its glow.
　It's a frustration
　And consternation.
It's evident Trump will need a furlough.

Day 76   11/5/2020

The pundits and reporters now report
Trump's numbers are coming up short.
   Like Tyrannosaurus Rex
   Trump will soon be EX,
Though the vote he continually attempts to distort.

Day 75   11/6/2020

It's an inordinate time in the count slow down
To determine if Trumpism will be a closedown.
    I hope not a precedent
    In selecting a president
To take such a long time for the final showdown

Day 74   11/7/2020

We know now that Biden is our new president-elect.
The Trump wrong headedness, we've chosen to reject.
With Harris on the team
Ahead it's full steam
As some blunders and mistakes they hope to correct.

Day 73   11/8/2020

Yesterday the world had a great celebration
Today Biden must move ahead in a collaboration
   And reach across the aisle
   With a genuine smile
Including everyone in our future destination.

Day 72   11/9/2020

Trump hasn't many options from which to
    choose.
There's a factual matter he chooses to refuse.
    The political factoid
    He'd like to avoid
Is the election, which he chooses to refuse to lose.

Day 71   11/10/2020

Attorney General Barr still supports his old Boss.
Boss Trump is still firing, despite his loss.
   It's pure nonsense
   To fire Secretary of Defense.
Firing Trump is the message to get across.

Day 70   11/11/2020

Trump won't accept the termination of his political line;
Former transitions have been gracious, sometimes benign;
Graham and Pompeo
And others also,
Avow that they agree with Trump's personal design.

Day 69   11/12/2020

Trump hasn't made the traditional concession speech.
Though he was able to survive the congressional impeach.
But despite his fraud claim
And his infamous name,
He's personally stretched as far as he can politically reach.

Day 68   11/13/2020

Trump continues to promote political division.
The election doesn't depend on his decision.
   He should quit;
   Take off his mitts.
He inspires only old politicians' derision.

Day 67   11/14/2020

Trump must now be given the admonition
That President-elect Biden is now in position
   For matters presidential
   And essential
To manage a smooth interregnum transition.

Day 66   11/15/2020

Trump tried desperately to get his presidency extended,
But the nation's worst leadership will soon be ended.
They'll drop the curtain
And we'll know for certain
That in 66 days Trump will be officially unfriended.

Day 65   11/16/2020

Obama still has a great deal to say:
Trump has contributed to "truth decay".
   He's playing games
   With his fraud claims,
Attempting to avoid the final play.

Day 64   11/17/2020

Trump had planned an attack on Iran.
Others had to dissuade him from his plan
   For armed conflict
   Then an edict
To stay and finish the war that he began.

Day 63   11/18/2020

Trump fired the official who dismissed the fraud
　　claim,
Still trying to find someone else to blame
　　For the election loss.
　　But still as boss
He'll cheat to win in this deadly serious game.

Day 62   11/19/2020

It seems that there won't be a smooth transition.
Trump sees the presidency as just another acquisition.
　Some went bankrupt.
　His methods were corrupt.
Actually, bordering on presidential treacherous sedition.

Day 63   11/18/2020

Trump fired the official who dismissed the fraud claim,
Still trying to find someone else to blame
For the election loss.
But still as boss
He'll cheat to win in this deadly serious game.

Day 62   11/19/2020

It seems that there won't be a smooth transition.
Trump sees the presidency as just another
    acquisition.
    Some went bankrupt.
    His methods were corrupt.
Actually, bordering on presidential treacherous
    sedition.

Day 61   11/20/2020

Trump is attempting a kind of political
    subversion
Of the democratic process by personal perversion.
    Let us here note
    That he ignores the vote,
Threatening war as an official election diversion.

Day 60   11/21/2020

Trump pulls from the hat a different surprise
Expecting millions of votes to be disenfranchised.
 Subverting the nature
 Of a state legislature
Pressuring them to give him the election grand prize.

Day 59 11/22/2020

Trump's election claims are based on mendacity
There's no accounting otherwise for his audacity.
It's then no surprise
When his claims are lies
That he's way in over his personal capacity.

Day 58   11/23/2020

Republicans say it's time to begin transition
    process,
And for Trump to give Biden appropriate official
    access
  To briefings and files,
  And cease the denials.
What Trump will do now, is anybody's guess.

Day 57   11/24/2020

Past reality we can't begin to dissolve.
To move ahead is our mutual resolve,
  And now advance
  To join the dance,
While the wheels of time continue to revolve.

As the transition now starts to advance
We choose our personal political stance,
  And then resolve
  As time revolves,
To make the future more than mere
    happenstance.

Day 56   11/25/2020

Trump is starting on a pardoning spree
Several criminals will be allowed to GO FREE.
  The first, Michael Flynn
  For him a big win
Maybe Trump's new show on reality TV?

Day 55   11/26/2020

We still wait to hear from Attorney Giuliani
Who adds his voice to Trump's cacophony?
   Subsequently to applaud
   The effort to prove fraud,
Exposing their own legal phony-baloney.

Day 54   11/27/2020

Trump won't promise to attend the inauguration,
Due of course to his massive self-infatuation.
   The attention on him
   Would be quite slim.
A simultaneous rally could continue his
     idolization.

Day 53   11/28/2020

Trump insisted the recount of Wisconsin's number;
A Trump attempt that proved to be another bummer.
There's no longer hidin'
That President-elect Biden
Won Wisconsin by an even larger number.

Day 52   11/29/2020

Amy Barrett professes pro-life claims.
How many people will Covid-19 maim
   To change her vote
   To revoke
Church attendance limits in this heavenly game?

Day 51   11/30/2020

A question we'd like to ask of an expert:
Did Trump's rallies help, or did they hurt?
　We still don't know
　About his political shows
But in business he at times lost his shirt.

Day 50   12/1/2020

Lara Trump is President Trump's daughter-in-law
She thinks Biden has plenty of time to withdraw
   And change the direction
   Of the recent election
And cover up Trump's crimes and family flaws.

Day 49   12/2/2020

Trump is considering pardons for his whole family,
And also, for his personal attorney, Giuliani,
Apparently realizing,
They've been capitalizing,
On information as official government employees.

Day 48   12/2/2020

Uncovered is a "bribes for pardons" scheme,
Not just for Trump's crooked government team.
　　Much has been redacted,
　　　But not yet retracted,
Shedding more light on Trump's self-serving regime.

Day 47   12/4/2020

According to Attorney General William Barr,
There's no credible evidence, at least so far,
 Of voting flawed
 Or Election fraud.
Trump's paranoia is incredibly bizarre.

Day 46   12/5/2020

Trump has completed a Pentagon purge
Of top officials, for his loyalists to emerge.
   He goes on a spree
   Wherever it may be,
And he wastes funds, as he continues to splurge.

Day 45 12/6/2020

The Pentagon blocked Biden's intelligence team
In order to enhance Trump's fraud election
   scheme;
For his power to extend.
And regulations suspend,
The danger being worse than at first it may seem.

Day 44   12/7/2020

A day of disaster: the Pearl Harbor attack!
Another disaster: this time a bushwhack
   On the election results
   Midst Trump's insults
Attempting to illegally force an election rollback.

Day 43 12/8/2020

Of the Georgia vote, Trump was not satisfied.
His legal court cases continued to divide
　Religions and racially
　And income especially.
But the election result in Georgia was certified.

Day 42   12/9/2020

After Trump what will happen to GOP?
He'll bring them to their political knees
  In supplication
  To our nation,
Birthing many new orange-haired wannabees.

Day 41   12/10/2020

Arizona Judge says Trump must follow the laws.
The last election lawsuit has too many flaws
 The flawed lawsuit
 But who gives a hoot?
Trump is paying for his personal Santa Claus.

Day 40   12/11/2020

Attention is gradually shifting to Biden et al.
Police reform seems slow for Biden to install.
   Despite the season
   There are reasons
And Trump is reluctant to hand over the ball.

Day 39   12/12/2020

The Supreme Court thwarts the legal blitz,
Despite Trump's and Texas's desperate hits
   To try to overturn
   The election returns;
So, we hope they'll finally call it quits.

Day 38   12/13/2020

Trump's lawyers' election challenge is shredded
By Justice Jill Karofsky, noting their case is headed
Down a path of innuendo
And thus, a crescendo
Of destructive actions in which they are embedded.

Day 37   12/14/2020

"We'll get Biden," says Alex Jones,
Making threats in belligerent tones,
   Giving a command
   And a demand,
Meaning nothing less than skull and crossbones.

Day 36   12/15/2020

Trump's lawyer, "Stock up on 2nd Amendment
    supplies."
More ominous than we may at first realize.
    It seems armed conflict
    Is what they predict.
Or is it just a loser's choice to fantasize?

Day 35   12/16/2020

Attorney General William Barr resigns
Trump still looking for his personal headlines
   The confessions
   Of Jeff Sessions
Revealed that Trump stepped over the personal line.

AG William Barr resigns
Justice Department had not found signs
   Of election fraud.
   Trump thought it odd
When Barr knew Trump wanted personal headlines.

Day 34   12/17/2020

A policy of the Trump re-election machine
Was deliberately to spread the Covid-19.
　It's unbelievable
　But could be conceivable
That it might be flushed down the GOP latrine.

Day 33   12/18/2020

From Mar-a-Lago neighbors for the New Year
To Trump, "We don't want you living here."
How can a loser
Be a chooser
When your neighbors don't even want you near?

Day 32   12/19/2020

Trump hasn't acknowledged the cyberattack
Is it for his friend, Putin, a convenient payback?
　The collusion stinks,
　And Romney thinks
The Kremlin wants Trump to stay on track.

Day 31   12/20/2020

Trump's challenges to Georgia's votes were
    denied.
His frivolous lawsuits, the justices just can't abide.
    He's quite disappointed
    With those he appointed,
But even they must admit, he has lied, lied AND
    lied.

Day 30   12/21/2020

Undeterred by earlier judges' court rejection,
Trump attempts to reverse Pennsylvania's
      election,
   Reversing the cases
   And the vote erases
To give the Assembly further election reflection.

Day 29   12/22/2020

When the cyberattacks are making a hit
Trump seems to be having his usual fit.
   He loses composure,
   As there is a disclosure
By intelligence officers that Russia is the culprit.

Day 28   12/23/2020

If martial law were declared in several states.
How could the new administration hope to
    extricate
  Trump's remaining
  And thus claiming
To have him declared the presidential designate?

Day 27   12/24/2020

Communism was caused by Twitter's censorship,
Says Trump, after he's received the pink slip.
  He was shocked
  That he was mocked
He has lost his grip on his royal leadership.

Day 26   12/25/2020

Looking for a gift under the Christmas tree,
Trump wants a gift-wrapped card to go free.
    Begging to receive
    An official reprieve.
He's been seen, sitting on St. Putin's knee.

Day 25   12/26/2020

Trump tromps the golf links at taxpayers' expense.
At Mar-a-Lago collecting for himself many dollars and cents.
  We are paying
  For his playing
Most of his actions now are pure nonsense.

Day 24   12/27/2020

Near the end of his quite visible presidential stage,
Trump behaves in a strange way to engage
    On the stimulus matter.
    And like the Mad Hatter
In his own Wonderland, chooses now to rant and rage.

Day 23   12/28/2020

Trump's pardons depend on payoff money.
That all involves obviously patrimony.
    They're giving him millions,
    While he claims to have billions.
His goodhearted favors are tainted baloney.

Day 22   12/29/2020

Twenty-two more days of Trump's insanity
As he continues to exhibit his life of profanity
   His days incline
   His crimes entwine
Though exceeded by his own narcissistic vanity.

Day 21   12/30/2020

2020 will be a year we're not likely to forget
Of course, Trump's shenanigans we already regret.
   We certainly recall
   That many of y'all
Voted for him, knowing his collusion with the Soviet.

Day 20   12/31/2020

2020 a year filled with presidential lies
A year when the majority of voters did realize
   That Trump was a lout
   So, they booted him out
Although millions were still mesmerized.

Day 19   1/1/2021

A few people were allowed to see the crystal ball,
In person in Times Square to see its annual fall.
   Year 2021
      Has begun.
Trump will soon be gone with his border wall.

Day 18   1/2/2021

A brand-new year and soon a new president,
New and quite different, which is really evident.
   Gone will be the unnerving
   Donald Trump, self-serving,
To be replaced by Joe Biden, my vote well spent.

Day 17   1/3/2021

Not cooperating with Trump is a group of seven
  GOPeers
He wants them to change the count of the
  electioneers;
  The official count,
  Which would amount
To Trump threatening them and their political
  careers.

Day 16   1/4/2021

Carl Bernstein says it's worse than Nixon's
  political Watergate.
Trump's attempted coup was with the Georgia
  Secretary of State.
The phone call was recorded
That fraud should be regarded,
But Republican Raffensperger refused to
  recalculate.

Day 15   1/5/2021

Georgians vote this time for two senators today
We'll just have to sit back to see what they say
   This post-election-election
   Will surely set the direction
To continue to fortify or file our fears away.

Day 14   1/6/2021

"Why does Trump want the job? He doesn't like the work."
Biden said of Trump, as Biden noted that Trump did shirk
   His responsibility
   For the probability
Of the spread of coronavirus that actually went berserk.

Day 13   1/7/2021

DAY OF INFAMY

What shall we say of January 6, 2021
When Trump's crime of sedition was actually done?
   In his opinion
   Of his minions,
They just came to Washington for some innocent fun.

They had done what Trump had urged them to do.
It was over when he told the rioters "I love you."
   It was their contribution
   To his angry retribution.
The charge of sedition will prove to be true.

Day 12   1/8/2021

There are times when reality is the nightmare.
It's more ominous when it's one that we share.
　　Yesterday's insurrection
　　Not just an imperfection.
Requires for awakening more than mere hot air.

Day 11   1/9/2021

Rioters were responding to an earlier Trump
   speech
Causing Congress and Pelosi to call to impeach.
   It won't be long
   Until he's gone
To impeach now may be an overreach.

Day 10   1/10/2021

There's a great deal of unrest in the nation.
In Washington there's much speculation
   About what is next
   In the context
Of Trump and his current political hibernation.

Day 9   1/11/2021

US Diplomats protest against Trump's protest,
In the countries where they are political guests.
  It's extremely difficult
  After our riotous tumult
To convince others that democracies are the best.

Day 8   1/12/2021

It seems that insurrectionists still plan an attack
On the Democratic legislators when they get back
　Like old renegades
　Setting up barricades
Allowing Republicans to save their megalomaniac.

Day 7   1/13/21

The Donald's legislative wall is beginning to crumble.
Even McConnell seems to be joining the rumble
Believing Trump's actions impeachable,
Now he is unreachable.
His senatorial support is taking a tumble.

Day 6   1/14/2021

The reason for Trump's second impeachment rejection
Was officially charged as "incitement of insurrection."
It was a fact
That he lacked tact
Accusing the Democrats of stealing the presidential election.

Day 5   1/15/2021

There was some dissension in Trump's political
    ranks
With much of their efforts showing only empty
    blanks.
  There were many
  Like Giuliani
For services rendered were offered nothing more
    than thanks.

Day 4   1/16/2021

The Trump regime will soon be over
When he will no longer need to hover
   Over his base
   To save face
And we won't need to run for cover.

Day 3   1/17/2021

The rioters were sure they had no need to hide,
As they had information which had been supplied
    By some policemen
    And congressmen
We know now they were insurgents on the inside.

Day 2   1/18/2021

Many of Trump's followers in the GOP
Are frightened and they're beginning to flee.
 To reiterate,
 His ship of state
Foundered in the uncharted Narcissus Sea.

Day 1   1/19/2021

The last official report to Trump has been submitted.
His political excuses and plots have become unknitted.
Upon losing his powers
He can retreat to his towers,
Until he is called to account for the crimes he has committed.

Day 0   1/20/2021

Trump didn't show up for Biden's inauguration,
He had hoped to get himself an exoneration.
   "All charity starts at home",
   And hiding his bald dome,
He retreated into a temporary hibernation.

Day 1   1/20/2021

Today, the presidency of Joe Biden has begun,
Counting the first 100, this being day one.
  I thought it only fair
  To give Trump some air,
Biden will jump start with the starter's gun.

After high school, E. Reid Gilbert pursued education from college to college, culminating in a PhD in Asian Theatre. He has won two Fulbright Awards. His careers have ranged from Methodist Minister to Mime, to Theatre (actor, director, producer and playwright) and University Professor. He is Professor-emeritus of Ohio State University. At the age of 80 he started a new career as an author and has published ten books plus ten plays. In addition to this book, he has three more manuscripts nearing completion: EMBODYING THE WORD; GESTURE WITH TEXT Movement Training for Actors: BEYOND THE POWER LINES AND PAVED ROADS, Memoirs of growing up in the NC tobacco hills; THE INNER LIGHT, a poetry collection.

www.ingramcontent.com/pod-product-compliance
Lightning Source LLC
Chambersburg PA
CBHW071003080526
44587CB00015B/2325